Murder Stay Murder

96/100

593 Vanderbilt Avenue, #265
Brooklyn, NY 11238

First Penmanship trade edition:

To contact Geoff Kagan Trenchard please visit
www.kagantrenchard.com/geoff
www.penmanshipbooks.com

This book is based on some true events,
however, they have been fictionalized
and all persons appearing in this work are fictitious.
Any resemblance to real people, living or dead is
entirely coincidental.

ISBN# 978-0-9831219-8-5
Library of Congress Control Number: 2012939614

Printed in The United States of America

10 9 8 7 6 5 4 3 2 1

For Em,
my beshert

The very emphasis of the Commandment:
Thou shalt not kill,
makes it certain that we are descended
from an endlessly long chain
of generations of murderers, whose love of murder
was in their blood as it is perhaps also in ours.

-Sigmund Freud

Another Matter Entirely

If you are talking
with an unfamiliar group of men
and everyone is sharing anecdotes
it is better that you tell them
that you have beaten another man half to death
than that you have loved one.

The story of the fight should have details lush
as the under side of a tongue. They'll want to hear
the dull knock when his head bounced
against the curb.
Did his face clench or just settle into your fist
like a catchers mitt? Was there a wet rip of skin
under your boots? Could you feel the scrape
of his teeth against your knuckles?

The story of loving a man
is another matter entirely.

If for some reason
you do end up talking about it, it
should always just be the fucking.
The act should have all the tender necessity
of an ATM withdrawal.
Just an off getting of rocks. A kinked nut
rubbed out. Do not talk
about the comfortable weight of his head
in your lap. The way his face held a goofy grin
and then fell to a calm slack. Do not claim
to know anything about the snug settle of hairy
leg over hairy leg. The soothe of being
on the receiving end of razor burn.

Even if you tell a very good story of the fight
it will not become your defining characteristic

unless you tell it many times.

This is not true if you say you have loved a man.
That's a story you only need to tell once.

Part 1. Mad in the blood.

All of us who are worth anything,
spend our manhood unlearning the follies,
or expiating the mistakes
of our youth.

-Percy Shelley

My first time all the way with a girl

was on the floor of my friend's squat,
under a patchwork of blankets and sleeping bags
zipped open flat. I remember the stubble
on her thigh as I peeled off her tights,
trying not to rip any additional holes
in them with my spiked dog collar bracelet.

Earlier that week in science class we watched
a movie, *The Miracle of Life*. There was a view
from inside a vagina of a full frontal penis.
It's circumference filled the twenty-four inch
screen. Inky flood of orgasm like sand clouds
around your feet when you walk on a beach
with water up to your knees. I remember
thinking,
THAT'S WHAT'S HAPPENING RIGHT NOW!

We had the same chin length black bob
with the sides shaved high. I remember
her eyes closed smile, but not her voice.
Her first name but not her last.

Waiting for the bus the next day, the sun
was so bright it felt sticky. I hadn't eaten,

and my bummed cigarette played hot dizzy in my
head. As I boarded, I thought
well, I guess I'm a man.
The air conditioning was turned up so high,
my sweat iced instantly. I pealed open
the mouth of my shirt and couldn't wait
for someone to ask me if I was a virgin.

The Hottest Places

I don't believe in hell
but Junior High gym class
did a great job of making me fear it.

Chris and I were part of the huff 40's and blunts
at lunchtime bunch. He had a jaw like a Jack
Daniel's bottle and a stepfather's temper.

I imagined his lips tasted like the cigarettes
I longed for through nic fitted detention.
It was an awful act of will to avert my eyes

from the bit of his hip peaking out
from his boxers as we changed each day
into our PE uniforms. I was acutely aware

of what would happen if I wasn't careful
about what I didn't do about it.
Even the implication of queerness

always drew blood.
The one out kid at my school was a red head
Mexican named Gabriel who flamed

like magnesium and had a locker in the same
bank as ours. On the day Gabe caught me
looking at Chris, rather then ratting me out

he flashed me a shrewd smile. Chris looked up
just in time to catch Gabe's grin. Decided
to defend my manhood with a battle cry of *faggot*

as if to ward off this disease.
I don't believe in hell, but if I did

it would smell like my Junior High locker room

during a fist fight.
Nothing says violence more desperately
than a thick cloud of cheap deodorant

that still doesn't cover the musk
of unchecked testosterone.
From where I stood I could see the gleam

of joy flash in the eyes of the crowd
with each dull thud. I didn't hate myself enough
to join in as Chris pounded his image

of masculinity into Gabe's face.
But I didn't care enough about Gabe
to do anything to stop it.

Eventually our dung beetle of a coach waddled
out of his office to break up the fight.
Then we all ran laps that lead nowhere

as a fat man with a clipboard
told us that if we stopped we were bitching out.
Gabe got marked down for getting blood

on his PE uniform. Chris offered
to split a cigarette with me once we got
to the far side of the field.

I held each drag till I got light-headed
even though they tasted like sulfur and brimstone.

Chuck

Double mocha. Extra shot. Extra chocolate.
No whip.Not too hot if you don't mind.
Beyond a regular, he is a moving fixture,
like the pile of ravaged newspapers
on top of the trash can. A shifting constant.
Slight shake of hand. Tremble in the leg. Rattle
of pills in their bottles. A phalanx of Russian tea
dolls. Each one just big enough to contain the one
to its left. If they were ever empty.
I've never seen them empty.
Lined up between him and the fancy glass mug
in which I serve him his coffee
always sits outside in the patio chair. Tearing
twelve sugar packets into forty eight perfect
squares. Apologizes for the mess.
When I go out to smoke he lends me
his lighter. The safety cap bitten off.
A smoking chain of Camel 100 Lights
around his right foot. Says he misses the drugs.
Not like these. Like drug drugs.
The Valium he takes now *would pack a buzz*
if they weren't barely numbing the stomach pain
from the Lithium. There's a dirty dozen others
whose names *I can't remember*
or pronounce. In rehab he made a three-page
single space list of all the reasons he had to stay
clean. Said *little sister. Not wanting my Mother*
to bury me. Save money. Half way down
the second page the seizures started.
First the hospital. Then a half way house.
Then he started hanging out here. He can't handle
a job, but gets disability. *It's enough to live on*
if you keep your life small. Chuck bends
the stir straws at every quarter inch. They coil

in front of the coffee. Which is in front
of the pill bottles. Which are next to the ant trail
of cigarette butts. In the center is Chuck;
arms folded and legs twitching. Asks me
did you ever make a fort as kid? Not like
in a back yard with scrap wood.
Like in your room with couch cushions
and blankets.
I give him back his lighter.
I say *yeah,*
I did.

My high school graduation

was in the middle of the football field. June sun
cooking us in our plastic caps and gowns, we
sweated like individually wrapped cheese slices
left out at a picnic. As the principal read the list
of seniors, his voice the same droll we heard
on every morning intercom,
I did my own accounting.

Pregnant friends filled one and a half hands.
Those in jail and/or rehab would have required
extra toes. The voice echoing through the stadium
gave no mention of Eric, who tried to hang
himself in the gym with a jump rope
over the basketball backboard. Or Bryan,
who snuggled the Tech 9 under his chin
after being expelled.

As we walked across the stage, they handed us
blank pieces of paper rolled in the style
of a diploma. Said the real thing
would arrive later in the mail.
Mine never did.

Almaden and Foxworthy

The day I moved in with Jen,
the boys who lived across the courtyard
helped me carry in my box-spring
as the fire department carried theirs out.

They ran around barefoot with PVC pipe swords.
A pair of make-believe centurions guarding
a half-empty pool. The burnt plastic smell
from blackened bathtub meth lab stank for miles.

This did not stop their parents from swearing
to the cops that they fell asleep with the iron on.
It looked as though the soot was dripping out
from their windows and up into the sky.

The only time I ever saw the landlord
was on his bi-weekly orbit around the mailbox,
searching for his Social Security check
like an antiquated satellite.

He had been at the complex so long,
the liver spots on his hands matched the
constellation of mold in my shower.
The day after the abortion,

the power was shut off.
We cried by candlelight. I thought more
about her ex-boyfriend than he will ever
think about me.

She said she didn't even really want him
that last time; it was just the easiest way
to get him to leave without a fight.
To look back on it now,

that whole chapter of my life is a dead star,
extinguished but still visible; proof positive
of my ability to see the world as flat if I want to.
I learned how fast a relationship

goes up in flames once you realize
you're only with someone because
their damage eclipses yours.
Jen gave me an easy out

when she picked a perfect day
for us to have our last argument.
The one thing nobody wants to hear
after being kicked to the ground

and spit on by Crips is that they aren't sensitive
enough to their partner's needs. I moved
everything I owned out in the middle of the night
on bruised ribs. My arms ached the same way

they did when I carried all this in. I took care to
step over the neighbors kid's Hot Wheels,
set around his older brother's broken forty
bottles. From above, it looked like

a miniature intersection, complete with accidents.

Of Copper and Chipped Teeth

Walking past people fighting
is like walking in on people fucking.
If you're unable to tell if it's personal or business,
it's best just to let the tangle bevel you away
like a wave. Don't think about the taste
of copper and chipped teeth, of nickel and panic.

Blood runs across his peach-fuzz mustache
and down around the chin like a burgundy goatee.
Gold teeth litter the street as two other youths sift
like claim jumpers and come up
with half a handful of nuggets apiece.

All men who render money from
war should be made to watch this:
kids too young to cash lotto tickets
painting a wall red with their palms.

He doesn't even have time to look up before
knees send him into the heavens,
fetal and benevolent.

I know how it is,
when the day you forget your knife
on the nightstand is the day he brings his boys,
and the fall to the ground goes slow as syrup.

How it is when they beat you
'til your nerves shriek curses.

To the blue sky refracted through spit that leaps
off lips a froth of *faggot* and *bitch*.

Curses to their parents' rotten cocks,
cunts and eyes. Curses

to every passerby,
may my horror
keep them up at night.

Curses to your clothes
as they attest defeat
down to their weave.

Curses to everything.
Except the cold concrete that holds you armless
and steadies your feet
until you can finally stand up
and leave.

27th and San Pablo

The Quarter-Pound Giant Burger across the street
from my apartment is a greasy beacon of light
that watches the liquor store close
and the crack den open.

This is where the still but furious grill
is the only thing that covers the smell
of half-spilled beers and piss,
of stale cigarette roaches and used-condom slugs
clogging the gutters. Perched alone
inside at the counter, there is a woman,
mini-skirt squeezing her chicken-skin
thighs like cellophane. Vinyl tube top
presses her breasts so hard against her chest
it cuts her cleavage like a loaf of bread.
This is where you hope
people aren't what they look like.

The lone cook on duty is a leathery prune
in a stained apron with wrinkles under his eyes
that claw down to his jaw. Out of the alley struts
a Mack truck in a do-rag. Thick neck
of a forty-ounce fit snug in his left hand.
A stride with the kind of fury that makes my fists
ball in my pockets. He runs right next to me
at the take-out window and shouts,
   THE FUCK YOU SITTIN' DOWN FOR?
She snaps,
I'm taking a break, Martin.

   Well you restin' on my investment, bitch.

*Well, maybe you need to quit making so many
deposits… bitch.*

He cracks knuckles wrapped in platinum.
They pop hollow in the cold air.
You have to wonder what it's like to come home
to a backhanded hello.
To get into a fight that starts because
you didn't order dinner to go, and ends
with a re-opened cigar burn on your shoulder.
For a second, she looks at me
like her boat's sinking
and I'm just standing on the dock.

Then,
                THE FUCK YOU STARING AT?
is shouted in my ear so loud, I feel it
more than hear it.

This is where a woman was found face-down
under an overpass the other night, a black plastic
bag from the corner store knotted around her neck
in a wrinkled scarf. I imagine a blade
cold as a railroad track sliding under my chin.
A motel mattress rushing up to my face
as it soaks my blood down to the box-spring.
Swallowing the knot in my throat I say,
Nothing.

Martin punches a window
like it owed him money.
But now he's gone and got the cook involved.
There is a steady hand moving under the counter
and the clap of metal gears as a round advances
to the chamber. This is where loud cracks
in the middle of the night
never mean a car backfiring. Where the tension
pulses in time with the neon sign.

Martin makes it my lucky night and backs down

the alley. Arms up in a vulnerable goal post,
bottle dangling in his grip
like an empty windsock, face
fixed to a high beam glare of
            Imo see you, later.
This is where I cross the street
to a warm, dry port. Count my change,
loose blessings, and can feel her gaze
follow me from the corner
as the deadbolt slides home.

The Ghost of Tony Montana
Haunts Martin Luther King Boulevard

Wakes up in the middle of the street
every evening at sunset, pinstripes crusted black
with dried blood. The last thing he remembers
is the slap of the water as he fell into the fountain.
Always charges the same route up the block.
Past the working girls skinny enough
to be his sister who all act like they don't see him.
Makes it to the intersection to turn left
on 123rd street. As he steps his guts churn out
a white shock. It drops him to his knees,
throwing up a pile of hot ash. After testing two
other corners Tony has to lay on the side walk
'til his legs stop their jelly wobble. Crawls to the
curb and sees a cornerboy with an oddly familiar
portrait embroidered over a leather jacketed heart.
Tony calls to him with a howl soft as free base
wind. It whistles up from Tony's punctured lungs
and out the holes in his bullet riddled limbs.
The boy chalks up the noise to an unfelt breeze.
It takes longer to forget about the shiver
up his spine. When Tony finally gets to his feet
he catches his reflection in the tinted window
of a Porsche that looks a lot like one
he used to own. The beads of sweat collect
and run an oil slick of filth down his face and on
to his lapel. He tries to recall the smell of the
store where he bought the white suit.
How the knot of hundreds in his pocket felt like
it added three inches to his dick. His scar begins
to give a wet and constant itch. An iron rake
of exhaustion runs across his bones. He stumbles
through the wall of a project building,
finds sanctuary in an apartment
that smells like his mother's pulled pork.

Lays down on the old woman's couch.
Watches her hide twenty dollars
between the pages of the family bible.
Her son steals it the moment
she goes into the bathroom
and he leavesthe front door wide open.
With his last grind of strength Tony gets up
to close it, turns the lock, and for a moment
is on a beach. Too young to know how poor he is.

Watching a wave crash and run to his bare feet.
As the blue on blue water touches his toes
he wakes back up in the middle of the street.

First day on the ward.

She is ambiguously ancient. Could be seventy.
Could be ninety. Grey hair bramble.
Low chin wattle. Wall eyes.
Veins bright blue as the medical bracelet.

> *I answer survey questions, but I want you*
> *should write in the paper for me.*
> *Begin.*

Do you ever have thoughts racing through your
head? Never? Rarely? Some of the time? Most of
the time? All of the time?

> *I used to work Macy's. Fifth Avenue*
> *perfume section. The man would say you*
> *have time to lean have time to clean.*
> *Never stand still. Good bottles*
> *do not have dust. I had best brown shoes.*
> *Shiny like mints but so comfy.*

I'll check rarely. Next question.
In the week before you came to the hospital
did you get along with your family members?
Always? Most of the time?
Half of the time? Rarely? Never?

> *My Herman is dead. Eighteen years now.*
> *Same camp as me, but we never met*
> *'til I live in Philadelphia.*
> *On South Street. In front of deli*
> *we would sit. He bought me spritz.*
> *Same camp for three years*
> *and never met till Leon's.*
> *Funny world huh?*
> *My children are grown*

but I see them for all the time they come
on holidays. My Sarah I love.
But she doesn't listen. Like she wants
I should be red in the face.

Eyes flush. Lip folds between strong teeth.
Breathes slow. I check most of the time.
Next question. Do you ever see things
or hear things that aren't there?

      Ach, what I smell in the city.
      On the subway. Stairs. I can't use.
      The elevator. Like boxcar. Like someone
      sick out of both sides at once. Here,
      I like. Smells like new books.
      Tomorrow I leave. They take me to home.
      I am too old to be here.
      Not like these people.
      Not head sick. Just old.

Hands nest in lap.
Turns loose wedding band round thin finger.

      Next question.

Have you ever thought you had special powers?

      Special powers?

Like you're invisible.
Or you can see through walls.
Or talk to god.

      Oh no. People say yes to this?
      You learn from these questions?
      This thing helps people?

Thank her for her time.
Wish her a nice day.
Note to self.

Sometimes.
Rarely.
Never.

Where did I get my sense of humor?

Being the only kid who celebrated Hanukah
in elementary school felt exactly like being the
only one who didn't believe in god at Synagogue.

> *What's the difference*
> *between a Jew*
> *and a pizza?*

My playground survival strategy
was to tell the joke's punch line
before the other kids did.

> *A pizza*
> *doesn't scream*
> *when you put it*
> *in the oven.*

At school, the Holocaust
was covered by one paragraph
in our two inch thick History textbook.

> *How many Jews*
> *can you fit*
> *in a Volkswagen ?*

At Synagogue, all the other kids
went to schools with uniforms
and had never heard any of my jokes.

> *Two in the front, two in the back,*
> *and six million*
> *in the ashtray.*

The last time I went to Temple I asked the Rabbi
how the Nazi's got away with killing so many
for so long without anyone noticing.

30

*Where were Jews
most concentrated
during world war two?*

I already had an idea about the answer.

The atmosphere.

2. War all the time.

War is a racket. It always has been.
It is possibly the oldest, easily the most profitable,
surely the most vicious.
It is the only one international in scope.
It is the only one in which the profits
are reckoned in dollars
and the losses in lives.

-Smedley D. Butler

Man's Ruin

Oh penis,
you are the looming overcast sky,
ninety eight percent humidity and a thunder
clap in the distance. There is no umbrella
that can protect me from the river of need
you drench. You lead the revolt
against my child body,
adamant red flag of insurrection
that would not be ignored in algebra class.
Had to tuck you under my belt like a tourniquet
to throbbing vein and walk with a hunch to hide
you. You, insatiable in your demands
for sacrifice. Constantly calling new
pornographies before the alter. You hijack
my eyes and make it so I can never look
at anything curved or anything straight
without the thought of you
somewhere in the picture.
A bargaining table with a time bomb centerpiece
is the best I get with us. I say, *just let me finish
the poem* and you look up at me with your
inhuman squint and reply
maybe.

Thursday, September 13th, 2001

I always liked the color blue. Calm as a bruise
after the swelling subsides. The color of bus
exhaust as it wafted past the cake of pigeon shit
stuck to the columns supporting the I-880
overpass. Cobalt neon of the bail bondsman's
office next to the Public Aid building.
The color of my work shirt turning to a shade
of cold skin from over-bleaching. It's wrinkles
shook from a dryer that ate my last
twenty- five cents. The pile of forms
thicker than my wrist I had to fill out
before meeting the social worker.
Federal on white paper, state on blue.
All the text was crooked.
Skewing to the left more and more
with each page. This was the year of the orphan.
The year a fireball burned day and night
on every television. The year my best friend
lost his mind. Powder blue eyes
only able to focus on his email death threats.
The year I folded everything into a Greyhound
ticket envelope. My pen ran out of blue ink
half way through the stack of papers.
No one could lend me another.

Gomer Pyle's rifle writes a love letter.

You were a perfect curvy section eight.
No way you had the granite heart
they sharpen here.

Should have been spit out
and sent home. A slab of fat
not worth it's gristle.

But your dumb luck got you joining
the big green killing machine
when it was running low on parts.

They beat you with bars
of soap until you were
born again hard.

You believed them
when they said this is all
just a bad dream.

Your eyes become cannon balls.
Devil dog snarl replaces
the jelly donut smile.

I see this all the time. The water
hardens in your veins. Start to wonder
what everybody looks like dead.

You have become
an animal mother
praying for war.

The killer instinct
is not an apple
you can unbite.

So I sing your bullets
so straight you can line
a bed sheet by them.

Let you think it's you
that shreds paper enemies.
Whisper promises

that hollowing out
the Drill Sergeant
will be just as easy.

They made you
a time bomb. I'm just
shortening the fuse.

Tonight your voice is clear
as a shell casing dropped
into a shallow puddle of water.

I know there is not much consolation
in knowing your death will save
at least as many lives as it cost.

So I will tell you this—
you look like royalty standing there
with your fist clenched behind your back.

Now show them
what one motivated Marine
and his rifle can do.

Finish turning
your face into a skull
and kiss me goodbye.

Back to the front

Over beer and seasoned curly fries
Matt tells me about the war.
How Iraqi street kids call the troops vampires
because of the eerie green-eyed glow
from their night vision goggles.

How they will in turn spit cherry Gatorade
and smile like a hacksaw. You have to keep it
tight on a patrol, he says. You have to
keep it tight. We lost touch after graduation.

He worked as a repo man and as an exterminator.
Joined the army because stealing cars legally
didn't have a medical plan for his son's asthma
and the spray used to kill roaches peals the skin
off your ankles in sheets.

He says roadside bombs aren't planted by anyone
in a militant group. Rather then risk their people
on something so small they pay
some non-affiliated citizen fifty bucks
that feeds a family of four for a month.

The recruiter said he'd be in Iraq for a year, tops.
When Matt had been there three
he got a dear john e-mail from his fiancé.
Now he's on his fourth refill of Xanaxs.
Army issue anti depressants are given out
in thousand count bottles. Because Matt is a
medic, his CO encouraged him to dole them out
however he saw fit.

In our Junior year he clicked up
with a crew of skinheads.
Said it was the only way a white boy

could walk around this neighborhood
with his chin up. I remember standing
in his bathroom doorway watching the clippers
spit hair off his skull. Asked what I should think
about him joining a club that's usually swung
at people like me. He said
as far as he was concerned, I was white enough.

So I became the punk
all the jocks wanted to jump
cause I dressed like a fag
but couldn't
because I was the Jew
who had a pack of skin head friends.

I buy the next round of shots and I ask Matt
if the guys ankle deep in blood and sand
think about the war. Says most of them know
they dying for profits they'll never see
and a people that don't want them there
because the country they swore to protect
needed someone to swing at.
Says even if there was a magic wand
that would bring all the boys home
with the ease of a credit card swipe
no one would use it.
As long as they're out there, he says,
we have to fight. As I sit
in this air conditioned bar,
looking at a parking lot full of unexploded cars
filled with expensive gasoline,
I am bereft of argument.

I know how ready for war Matt looked
in his straight laces and number one crop.
How he would sing along to my Smiths tape
when no one else was around.

How he once fended off fifteen Norteños
with a skateboard and knife that had a swastika
carved in the handle and cried when his friend
got kicked face first into a barbwire fence.

I don't ask if he still believes that white people
are some how more on his side.
When we leave here
he will still be locked
into a uniform I am again unable
to talk him out of.

Atticus Finch cuts a switch
for Alberto Gonzales

When the towers fell, I spat blood too.
Remembered the way my father

talked about the day
the Yankees torched Atlanta.

Had no love for the Confederacy but joined up
with all the other boys in town to bury a hatchet

in Lincoln's neck. I know what it is to see froth
on the lips of men who threaten your children.

To let someone get away with murder
for a greater good, we all compromise.

You don't strike me as the type
to start the lynch mob but you'd get up

from your bar stool and pick up a stick.
An attorney lying on the witness stand

doesn't just disgrace the speaker,
it whittles the pillars of our whole profession

down to tooth picks. Forget about the good-
looking seersucker suit, the knife twist

of courtroom theatrics. To practice law
is to bring divine reason onto the world

as if God were watching.
Even if he's not.

It is the scale on which we test

the validity of our civility;

this thing is not a knuckle-duster
for the Leviathan.

Not a throne that conforms
to whatever ass is in it.

Not a receipt we write after the bullet
is lodged in the dissidents head.

I can answer my children as to why
I bent my principles to favor mercy.

What will you tell yours?

Authorized Interrogation Techniques

Say hold head immobile.
Spread fingers
slightly apart.
Insult slap.
Do not allow repositioning of hands or feet.
Finger tips supporting all the body's weight.
Legs fully extended
for up to forty consecutive hours.
Say reduced caloric intake.
Manipulated room temperature.
Deprivation of sleep.
Left to stand naked in a cell for months.
Use of blindfold.
Earplugs.
Diapers.
Strapped to stretcher.
Say restraints.
Dog collar.
Desecration of holy scriptures.
Live insects placed inside the confinement box.
Water poured on a cloth wrapped around the
mouth and nose.
Say simulates drowning.
Say sense of suffocation.
Say suffocation of sense.
Say let's roll.
Evil doer.
Jack Bauer.
Say only four hours? I stand on my feet all day.
Say what if they had a bomb?
Say what if it was your son was in the building?
Say what if it was your son in the uniform?
Say what if it was your son in the chair?

South of Heaven

In the tedious stretch between 11 am and 4 pm
at the AT&T store Thomas remembers
the things he's done. The weight of the chain
is in his hand again. Leading the enemy
combatants by five point restraints to the
processing room, they strip naked under a bare
bulb as Slayer blasts over the PA, as if Satan
himself was screaming at them. After the hospital
smocks and blind hoods, Thomas moves them to
their cells. The Lieutenant never has him
do the heavy work. It isn't him
with the collapsible baton or guard dog.
His job is to assist. To inflate the rubber glove
for the sissy slap. To refill saline IV
and mop up the piss. Once a week, rearrange
the wall of blue teeth and car adapters.
The schedule in the break room is written
in the same handwriting as the one hung
in Building 2. All the bills in his register
face the same direction.

The night before he shipped out, all the members
of his band got matching pentagrams tattooed
on their left shoulders. Stayed up all night
sucking iced bong rips with South of Heaven
cranked to eleven and on infinite repeat.
Around 3 in the afternoon, the opening chords
get stuck in his head. He runs out to his car.
Smokes a cigarette down to the filter. Presses
the hot cinders into his arm until they go wet.
Every surface of the store gets a Lysol
and Windex wipe down. Thomas' boss likes him.
Appreciates that he finds himself
little cleaning projects when it gets slow.
His formal long sleeves, even in the middle

of the summer. Never bothers him
about the occasional unscheduled break.

50 seconds in the life of a killer.

*We did it for fun. It was fun to see a system
that has so much power and control lose it
in a second.
That day...was the most fun I have had
in my entire life.*
- Kayson Pearson at his trial
for the rape and murder of Romona Moore

1. She's in the basement.
2. Need to go to the store.
3. Garbage bags.
4. Breakfast at the diner.
5. Treat myself to extra bacon.
6. Take my time 7. I can't stop smiling.
8. First the duct tape. 9. Then the knife.
10. I never take my shirt off.
11. Brought the Playstation downstairs.
12. Knife again. 13. Cigarette down to the filter.
14. Flick. 15. Cry all you want. 16. No one is
listening. 17. Turn up the music. 18. *At my
arraignment, note for the plaintiff. Your
daughter's tied up in a Brooklyn basement.*
19. Sing it. 20. I said sing it.
21. Wire cutters 22. Duct tape.
23. Do you want to see how strong I am?
24. Barbell. 25. Hard day's work.
26. Sleep tight. 27. The sun through my window.
28. Need to go to the store.
29. Carton of cigarettes.
30. More bags. 31. In the aisle.
32. Something's not right. 33. The rows
of detergent.34. Something's not right. 35. Cunt
cashier. 36. What are you looking at?
37. Just leave. 38. On the sidewalk.
39. Something's not right.

40. Can't breathe. 41. Why can't. 42. I feel. 43.
My hands? 44. Almost home. 45. You're gonna
get it now. 46. Why won't. 47. My hands. 48.
Stop 49. Sound of the sealant pealing away
as I open my front door.

The ongoing list of things I have learned from murderers.

On one of our many cut school bus rides, #1 said
a girl had been raped. Her brother had three grand
and a mind to do something about it. He bought
yellow kitchen gloves and a new aluminum
baseball bat. Got an address he staked
out for days to wait for the first new moon.
Says a skull sounds exactly like a softball
when hit hard enough. At a writing workshop
in San Quentin, #2 told me that the gunfight
could have been choreographed by John Woo.
Burned his clothes when he got home,
but there wasn't a drop of blood or scorch
of powder got on them. #3 explained
that if a drug deal "goes bad" it looks nothing
like the movies. Soon as someone draws,
everyone scatters. Inching his way out
of the warehouse, a cleaning woman sneaks up
on him. Shoots her dead before his eyes
have time to focus. #4 described a similar story
in the sparse poem nervously read at an open mic.
In Baghdad, a thirteen year old boy put a 7.62mm
hole in his shoulder. #4 dropped two .45 caliber
slugs in his head. When he gets off stage I try
to shake his hand. He looks at the floor.
#5 was cracked out of his mind in a country
most people only see on commercials
for Save the Children. Cop kills his friend.
Leaves the body folded in a sewer pipe.
One forty-ounce bottle filled with gasoline burns
down a house a lot faster then you might expect.
Doesn't see the tricycle in the front yard
till it leaves his fingers. I changed the title
from "An incomplete list" to "The ongoing list"
when #5 texted me that #6 smothered an invalid

woman in a nursing home. He was working off
the books and had a migraine that wouldn't let
up. No one seems to know any more than that.
There was a summer when the murder rate
and temperature in Oakland hovered
around a hundred for two weeks.
The night the rain broke, seven people were killed
within a block of my apartment.
None of the incidents were related
except for time and place.
Even after I move away
the bodies form a perfect crescent
around my door.

Drug Czar

I come from a family where getting fucked up
is an inherited recipe. Anything I didn't learn
from a grandmother who drank herself to death
on cheap vodka and food stamp tomato juice,
I picked up from my cousin who chopped speed
with a drywall knife 'til his knuckles splintered
like fiberglass. There wasn't much new
for Officer Weber to tell me when he came
to my seventh grade Social Studies class to tell us
about the D.A.R.E program. I distinctly
remember how Officer Weber paced the length
of the chalkboard, slapping his basketball of a gut
in time with the pregnant pauses of his sentences.
    Well, kids,
his thick fingers palming
both sides of his stomach like Buddha molesting
his own belly,
        I'm here today, to talk to you,
        about the dangers
        of amphetamines.

The first time I did speed was about
a week before. Mike dropped an eightball
into our Super Big Gulp.
We stayed up 'til sunrise smoking endless
cigarettes, meticulously duplicating album covers
on our notebooks. A few years later,
Mike went to jail for burglary.
Took a vocational course on how to cook
diet pills with gasoline for fun and profit.

One day, Officer Weber played a movie intended
to relate to us on our level. You know the story:
a troop of bubble-headed teenieboppers get
approached by a shady figure

who tries to get them hooked on "the dope."

Before my friend Lisa became a statistic
used to scare parents, she sat at the desk
next to mine in home room. Once let me watch
while she changed her shirt when we ditched.
I never got to kiss her, but she gave me
her pewter skull necklace with the knife
in its head and plastic ruby eyes.
Over Christmas Break she whittled herself
down to a skeleton in heavy mascara.
The last time I saw her was in hospital room.
Said the day she gets out she's catching
a Greyhound to Missouri. Meet up with a boy
who loved her enough to tattoo her name
over the abscesses on his shooting arm.

At the end of my seven weeks
of Drug Abuse Resistance Education,
we had a party with juice boxes and popcorn.
Officer Weber handed out ribbons yellow
as a streetlight in an empty lot, that read
PROUD TO BE DRUG FREE.
The acid I took at lunch was just kicking in.
His voice sounded like the shriek of air
from an emptying balloon as he congratulated me
and placed his award on my desk.

Part 3. How do you plead?

It's real spooky like a real trife movie.
Remember the part
where Terminator killed Tookie?
Absolute power corrupts absolutely.

-MF DOOM

In the Cannabis Club

In the back of a coffee shop the walls are papered
ceiling-to-floor in 12-inch LP covers.
Kurt Cobain sits to the right of Biggie Smalls,
like the heaven so many stoners dream of.
I'm so high I can hear the termites in the walls
chomp to the tune of Big Poppa.
Through the haze is Michael, trying
to be as unobtrusive as possible, but the bulk
of his electric wheelchair wedges
between the plastic tables like an R.V.
in a drive-thru. I would not go so far
as to say we're friends, but definitely nodding
acquaintances. I would notice if I never saw him
again. His cerebral palsy forces his bones
to corkscrew into his muscle, makes his skin
crinkle like wet papier-mâché; his chest, a Mylar
party balloon slowly sinking inward as it runs out
of air. This is in sharp contrast to the seamless fit
of his Adidas jumpsuit. 35% cotton and 65%
polyester have never looked this good together.
And the shoes, the holy grails of shell toes.
Somewhere a young B-boy prepares a paste of
409 and Windex that will be applied with an
extra-soft toothbrush, with a dream
of kicks like these. Michael speaks in a wisp
forced over lips that move as if they're numb.
A crooked coral reef of pearly white teeth
attached haphazardly to his gums.
In his left fist, he scrunches a Zippo.
It's swollen to nearly twice the size of his right.
Extends a crooked index finger
and tries to spin the wheel.
The first couple of strikes are unsuccessful.
I can see tension shriek white under his

fingernail. He tries again with a determination
that could crack a diamond. I hesitate
offering a light. Afraid it would come off
like I think he needs my help. I want to be
described as "well-intentioned"
about as much I want to gargle bong water.

Finally, the lighter flashes. The tip of his blunt
glows like Rudolph's nose, his tongue now a tide
he can finally control. Michael puts down
the lighter, asks if I want to hear a joke.
I say, sure.

> How do you get a one-armed
> hippie out of a tree?

I don't know.

> Pass him a joint.

No Homo Ghazal

Not that there's anything wrong with that
is the same chicken shit side step as *no disrespect*
intended or *I swear not to come in your mouth,*
no homo.

Hip hop just has the balls to drop
onto the palm of the modern lexicon,
no homo.

At some point every man learns
you gotta be the biggest dick in the room
to not get fucked,
no homo.

Gentlemen, you cannot let a sound run
over your lips that does affirm the rock hard
nature of your identity,
no homo.

Erect a panopticon in your throat
as if the world had a flashlight up your ass,
no homo.

I am the last person to tell you
that it is safe in a man's skin,
no homo.

How I knew

We met at a poetry slam.
Said she loved my metaphor
using the Pythagorean theorem
but thought I had robbed Mr. Rogers
for his sweater.

At our take out dinner date
said she didn't trust people
who have never considered suicide
and made fun of the way I held my chopsticks.

When I told her it was because
I'm developing arthritis.
She blushed,
but did not apologize.

Later that night
we were talking about her friend
that died in a plane crash.
Said she would never forget

how little attention she paid
to the news report that played
in the background
just before she got the phone call.

The next morning she tried to tuck
her splashing smile into her shoulder
when I squeezed her hand
as we walked down the street.

Powder Burn

Not that I consider myself a dealer per se.
Just an enthusiast of vice that always seems
to have the phone number you're looking for.

So I get a call from a high-strung art student
that lives in a neighborhood with blood spots
on the sidewalk but in five years

will have a juice bar. Black and white
cop cars drag past the oversized white tee's
reflected in chrome searchlights and aviator

sunglasses. Down the curb stomps a woman
with half a weave blooming out her head
in a frozen red mist. I duck into a 24 hour

Donut Shop/Take Out spot with a pocket full
of good times and bad news to wait for the call.
In the one booth sits a man entirely comprised

of pockmarks, Dickies and Old English lettering.
His girl is perched next to him, her lacquered
talons pet a lap dog. Its car alarm bark snaps

at the raggedy chorus of twitching faces.
They stand in a politely strung out clothes line
cross the restaurant. Patiently waiting

for the blessing of a handshake. Begging
appraisals for baby clothes and silver tarnished
brown as a bear claw. Wonder if the customer

I'm waiting on will ever be too broke
to get his drugs delivered. In these situations
it's best to keep your eyes to your self.

Focus on the glass case and its militant row
of pastries. It is there I catch the contorted
reflections of two cops as they walk in.

One white and one black, young enough to be
either very cool or very not. For white people
involved in the drug trade, there are no questions

regarding the existence of racial profiling.
It is as blatant as the sunrise over a cocaine
hangover. Everybody knows

why you're squinting. My eyes fix on the Old
Fashions and I breathe steady. The Cholo
looks at the cops like they're a windshield

he would love to break his hand on. His girl's
snarl could make battery acid flinch,
eyes locked on the black cop.

The white cop gives me a polite nod
as I walk outside to answer my phone.

Hymen Roth's Advice for Bernie Madoff On The Day of His Sentencing.

There is an alley in Manhattan
where I once threatened
to burn a woman's lips off.
We got her alone and held a sewer rat
by the neck. Rubbed its face
in cleaning powder from the tire factory.
When the fur started to sizzle
I knew she wouldn't
press the charges.
I was not happy to do this thing,
but you can't have loose talk
where business is concerned.
Until very recently
the spot was an office
for a bankrupt savings and loan.
Think on this when the prosecutor
looks at you like it's only Jews
who bleed green.
Don't let them
sons of bitches act
like crime don't pay.
The only difference
between a button man
and a badge man
is who they call for back up.
The courtroom where you sit
was built by Micks and Wops for pennies.
Sits on the graves of Shvartzas and Squaws.
When you get to prison,
if you bribe the right guards
they take care of you.
All money has at least some blood on it.
In a large pile it will stink like a corpse.

Lesson Plan

The day after Obama got elected
I went to Rikers Island
to teach a poetry workshop.
No one sent them the memo
that we are now living in a post racial society.

I went to Rikers Island
to teach a poetry workshop
dressed like a substitute English teacher.
We are now in a post racial society,
the uniform for hip white people is jeans
with a collared shirt and no tie.

Dressed like a substitute English teacher
the guards looked at me like I was a joke
that needed no set up.
The uniform for hip white people is jeans
and a collared shirt with no tie.
Warned me with a smile
   'round here they serve chilidogs
   to boys like you.

The guards looked at me like I was a joke
that needed no set up.
The workshop was canceled
but no one would say why.
Warned me with a smile
   'round here they serve chilidogs
   to boys like you.
This was not the first time.

The workshop was canceled
but no one would say why.
On the bus ride home I thought about the damp
shellfish smell of cold.

59

This was not the first time.
Nothing moves quickly in a prison
unless an alarm is going off.

On the bus ride home I thought about the damp
shellfish smell of cold.
Thought about all the different uniforms
waiting in the lobby.
Nothing moves quickly in a prison
unless an alarm is going off.
Decided to wear my best suit from now on.

Thought about all the different uniforms
waiting in the lobby.
Noticed how anyone with a briefcase is called *sir*.
Decided to wear my best suit from now on.
Shined shoes and a bright tie.

Noticed how anyone with a briefcase is called *sir*.
Now all the guards looked at me
like I was a pay lawyer.
Shined shoes and a bright tie.
My teaching partner said
> *I passed as perfectly legitimate*
> *white person.*

All the guards looked at me
like I was a pay lawyer.
I even got a friendly nod from the warden.
My teaching partner said
> *I passed as perfectly legitimate*
> *white person.*
This time we managed to get into a classroom.
I even got a friendly nod from the warden.

The class was cut from an hour
down to ten minutes.

This time we managed to get into a classroom.
Above the door it read,
> *Safety is the primary concern*
> *of this institution.*

The class was cut from an hour
down to ten minutes.
So I tried to start a conversation
about race in the media.
How above the door it reads,
> *Safety is the primary concern*
> *of this institution.*

All the pencils had to be collected
before they could be used.

I tried to start a conversation
about race in the media.
No one sent them the memo that
all the pencils had to be collected
before they could be used
the day after Obama got elected.

The wax bullet tweets.

A solemn day. Barring a stay by Sup Ct, & with my final nod, Utah will use most extreme power & execute a killer. Mourn his victims. Justice

-Mark Shurtleff, Utah Attorney General, via TwitBird
referring to the firing squad execution
of Ronnie Lee Gardner.

I am dud. Plug shuffled in with the real deal.
Chance one of the five executioners won't be.
I am giver of good sleep. #Plausibledeniability.

No struggle as they lead him. Clamped to the
black throne. Resting place for the wicked. 7 sand
bag each side. Paper circle pinned on chest.

They are good men. Professional. Calm. As if
returning a defective product to the manufacturer.
They each get a commemorative coin. #Nojoke.

He can't see us. Just slits in far wall. Moat of
light gouges cold room. Any last words? Thumb
twitch. Black hood cinches. Neck vein throb.

Some born to sweet delight, some born to endless
night. rt@wblake. This one pulled out of mothers
womb, dropped into his brothers crotch.

Some will ask for blood atonement. Some will
dissolve mid flight. Flesh shall be delivered unto
Satan unto the day of redemption. #livebygun

Countdown cadence started. They said he
watched the LOTR trilogy last night. Say they
play Freebird for him outside.
gtg.5432isthelonelest#.

How the guidance counselor used his words today.

My principal pulled me aside
first thing this morning.
Used the words
police, *question*, and *student*.
I used the words
which and *why*.
He used the words
weapon and *automatic*.
We both used the words
hope, *ditch*, and *today*.

Half way though second period,
the student arrived at my office.
He used the words,
my and *bad*.
I used the words,
hurry and *Algebra*.
He used the words
thanks and *peace*.

I picked up the phone
and used the words
here and *now*.
I picked up the phone
and used the words
son and *precinct*.
For the rest of the day
I didn't say much.

The rules of on screen engagement

If the hero is a white man
he can kill anyone
who has wronged him.

In addition,
he can kill everyone
who happens to be near by

provided they don't
have any lines
of dialogue.

A white woman can kill
but only in defense of herself,
her children, or her man.

If she kills
for any other reason,
she cannot be the hero

and must be punched
in the face at least once
by another white woman.

A black woman will rarely kill
as hero or villain, but will always
say something funny in the first act.

A black man can only kill
something more black or monstrous
than himself

and must say something funny
soon after he does it.

The Making of a Socially Acceptable Sociopath.

On August 1st, 1966, Charles Whitman
lugs half a dozen hunting rifles
to the University of Austin clock tower.
Jack Scagnetti is five years old.
Steals a pack of Double Mint Gum
into the holster of the Davey Crocket cap gun set
he wears everywhere except to church.
His Mother catches him as they leave
the drug store. Drags his ear through the town
square stopping every few feet to scream on him
like it was the worst thing he had ever done.
Jack cries harder then the last time
he wet the bed. Thinks about what would happen
if she finds the shoebox with the half dead mouse
he keeps behind the shed. Jack slips out of her
grip just before the first of Charles' shots collides
with her hip. Folds her in half fast as a chopped
corn stalk. In a puddle of ballooning blood, her
out stretched arms meet dilated eyes.

The second shot catches her square in the chest.
Sends her hands into a flattened hosanna above
her head. When Jack grows up he will not
remember this pose when he pins an old Black
man spread eagle over the hood of his squad car.
Nightstick lancing first the hip then sternum
while Jack's smile shines searchlight bright.
There will be no spark of recognition when he
duct tapes a young prostitute's wrists to a motel
headboard. The only thing Jack will remember
about this day is how good it felt to level
his gun at the clock tower and squeeze the trigger.

The man he intended to shoot

He is sick to his stomach and wants to vomit
because he just shot a man he did not intend to
shoot.

-Michael L. Rains, defense attorney for Johannes
Mehserle commenting on the video footage
of Mehserle shooting Oscar Grant in the back
while Grant is hand cuffed and face down
on a train platform.

The man he intended to shoot was not a man.
Did not gurgle and weep as he died.
The man he intended to shoot was a prop.
The man he intended to shoot would have made
him famous. He would have shot the man
and freed the woman and protected the town
and halted the invader and won the hearts
and won minds and won the big game
and saved the whole world.

The man he intended to shoot had no bed.
No kitchen. No shower curtain that needed
cleaning. No toothbrush. No favorite spot
in the break room. No preference how he took his
coffee if your going out for some thanks.
Had no hat and no coat that looked just like a
million others but smelled only like him.

Dirty Harry speaks to a 6th grade classroom at Througood Marshal Elementary

Every day, he kicks himself a little harder
for not retiring when the house was still worth
something. He could be on a boat facing a setting
sun. Instead, it's a white knuckle ride toward
mandatory retirement. Praying the pension
will still be there when he crosses the line.

So he's here. Where it is exactly as awkward
as you imagine. The commissioner said two
community outreach visits per week,
so it might as well been written in the 10
commandments. There was a clearly bullet
pointed memo listing what could and could not
be said. He starts off with his spiel about the
paperwork he never bothers with. The students
are off screen stares while they text under desks,
but one girl in the front row with a raised hand
is an open palm protest.

Mr. Callahan, you ever kill anybody?

The red and black beads woven into her hair
are a wave the rest of the class has just perked up
to crest. The teacher looks up from last weeks
grading ready to carpet bomb the whole room
in shush. Harry remembers how it used to be.
How even in the tender loins of the city
kids this age were at least a few years older
before they could tell who fired the shots
by how many seconds between each crack.
When not so many boys in a class like this would
have something lethal in a shoebox at home.
His sneer that could strip the varnish

off a foot locker dilutes to neutral.
He knows the next time he sees her
it's likely to be though a Plexiglas reflection,
or bloody. There is no harm
in telling the truth today.

Yes, young lady, I have.

When I posted the poem about the Junior High locker room fistfight on Facebook

I didn't think much about it.
It was up there with the YouTube videos
and a dozen other poems.
Hideous snap shots of my teenage incarnation.
Up there with the You Tube videos
the people are no longer real people,
just hideous snap shots from my teenage
incarnation. Ghosts in the attic
that make my floors creek.
The people, no longer real people.
Then I got an email from wonderlust_79.
A ghost in the attic made my floors creek,
when she asked if Chris was the kid who never
took off his Giants hat.
When I got the email from wonderlust_79,
I said no, he's a composite. A real feeling
given a fake name. When she asked if Chris
was kid who never took off his Giants hat,
I asked about the current state of the actual
Gabriel, who was not a composite, a real feeling
left with its real name. The screens glow
became a deluge. I asked about the current state
of the actual Gabriel. The words *died from aids,*
in the screens glow, a deluge.
A lesion budding on my tongue. The words
died from aids. The apology I was holding
behind my teeth became a lesion budding
on my tongue. I had convinced myself
it was like magic. All the apologies I hold behind
my teeth, just poems I have yet to write.
Fooled my self into thinking I was magic
Could find absolution if I just wrote it right.
The poems I have yet to write
becoming clouds of soot in my lungs.

Absolution for which I have no right.
They say the hottest places in hell,
(clouds of soot I carry in my lungs)
are saved for those who stood by doing nothing.
The hottest places in hell are earned by inaction.
Standing by. Watching. Doing nothing.
I carry a cancerous specter earned by inaction.
All my poems carry cancerous specters
that until now, I didn't think much about.

4. Tooth for a tooth.

The strategic adversary is fascism.
The fascism in us all,
in our heads and in our everyday behavior,
the fascism that causes us to love power,
to desire the very thing
that dominates and exploits us.

-Michel Foucault

Ars Poetica

When the boot
is about to collapse
your ribs,

the bag of dope already cut
and fluffed, the well
of sodden lust

boiled to burst,
it is both too late
and too soon for the poem

to help.
It can only,
on it's best day,

answer the nameless ring
that comes
after the gun is shot.

What I learned while teaching workshops in Rikers Island

If you are early enough to catch Regis and Kelley
On the waiting room TV, you know the gods
that govern the Q100 bus have shined on you
today. If you are still sitting in the lobby when
Maury tells the man in his church clothes he's
the father, there is something wrong
with your paperwork. If you are sent to under 21
building you are in luck. They much more likely
to be interested in what you have to say.
If the Officer has a Muslim name
or is openly wearing any sort of religious
paraphernalia, also luck. They are much more
likely to be interested in what you have to say.
If you are in the day room there is likely to be tee
shirts and sox drying on the plastic chairs.
The tables tell a mystery story in stains.
Chewing gum smeared black as soot.
The rust colored dust of Ramain packets.
If an inmate introduces himself by asking
what Crackin, he is a Crip. What's Poppin,
Blood. If the scar on his face is a straight line cut
down to the white meat, it did not come from
falling off a bicycle. If the poem you brought
for the lesson contains some amount
of sex, drugs, or violence, it's likely to go over
well. If it is written in a font size of less than 10
points, it will not. If asked to describe the smell
of a thing they cannot forgive, and some one says,
fresh rain in summer, thank him for sharing.
The feel? *Strange object in the mouth.*
Thank him for sharing. The taste?
A full glass of cold blood. Thank him for sharing.
Only talk about these images in abstract.

What they could hypothetically imply.
Never name names. Only write people's initials.
Act as though anything said can be used in court.
If they want to know how to find you when they
get out, say they can put your name into a search
engine. On the last day, even if you did all
you could, know there are 3 other rooms in this
building and 5 other buildings in this jail
and 10 other jails on this island
and a million other islands in this world.

Untitled

At night, the blue sky moves
to where it is needed most.
Every morning I am thankful
that it comes back around.

The first thing that ever really scared me
was the wax ball of minutes
that grew in my mouth
when I waited to be picked up.
Every second made me more sure
that no one was coming to get me.

In my head there is a plastic bolder
hovering above a flowerbox.
The only thing that holds it back
is the smallest wooden door stop.

This morning, the shower
had just enough hot water
to get me in, but not enough
to keep me there for long.

When I came back into the bedroom
You were curled around the good pillow.
Smiled like it was still the weekend.

I want you to know that I quit smoking
because you threatened to leave me
but I stayed quit because I wanted
to grow bigger than a sculpted shadow.
I want you to know that I think about
babies in a very non-abstract way these days,
that I feel safe leaving before you in the morning.
I'm almost 100% sure the blue sky will be
waiting for me.

The masturbation session
that stands out most to me

I was around thirteen and deep
into research as to the ideal lubricant.
Had always heard jokes about the smell
of Vaseline. Such a rarely used item
in my mother's linen closet, I reckoned
its absence would go totally unnoticed.
It didn't take long to develop
a shimmering coat. Right in the middle of things,
my Dad starts banging on my bedroom door
about some garbage or dish related infraction.
I closed up shop, but even after a thorough wipe
from yesterdays tee shirt my hand
was too saturated in petroleum
to get the friction necessary to turn the lock.
The night before, I was caught
on a playground at midnight.
Drunk howling my rendition of Jimmy Page's
solo from the 25 minute version
of Dazed and Confused. When the cops
brought me home, the lush of wine
stolen from his liquor cabinet
stained my lips beyond all explanation.
Even at the time I recognized the hilarity.
My Dad, kicking in the hinges,
convinced I was involved
in a completely different kind of malfeasance.
The panic crackle in my voice as a swore
I'll be out in a second!

It was the day the lock came off.

The first time all the way with a guy

was New Years Eve.
I had seen him around
the circuit of bars

I either worked at
or drank at.
Noticed the lack

of pause in his smile.
There was a warehouse party.
A glass coffee table

supported by the antlers
of a stuffed deer.
Lines of coke

long as the distance
from his ear lobe to his chin.
At some point

I decided
he was cute
enough to holler at

but too dumb to date.
Which made him perfect.
When we got back

to my apartment
He complimented me
on my lack of clutter.

I put on the *Madvillian*
album and rolled a joint.
By the time *America's Most Blunted* came on

I had my legs around his shoulders.
Of all the contortions
we twisted our bodies

into that night
the only thing
that made me

uncomfortable
was the thought
that he might figure out

what I hadn't
done before.

They are action figures, not dolls.

There will always be a leader
and several specialist who follow him.
Some are smarter. Some are stronger.
But they are not the leader.
The leader will most often be wearing red,
sometimes blue, but never any secondary color.
The specialists that follow him will be different
colors reflecting their skills. Orange is fire
and sunlight. Green is will be magic
or technology. The color will coordinate
with their skin if human and who their skin
represents if are not.

Some of them can be she's, but never
the majority. The leader will always be a he.

The leader will have an enemy leader.
The enemy leader will be a he too. This leader
always looses at the end of the cartoon, unless
the cartoon is in two parts. At the end of the first
part, he will appear to be winning
but then his arrogance will get the best of him
and he will make a mistake at a critical time.
Give a speech instead of throwing the switch.
Laughing manically instead of pulling the trigger.

One of the leader's followers will escape from a
dangerous situation. One of the enemy's
followers will fall down to make you laugh.
There will be lots of shooting that doesn't kill
anyone. There will a run toward the screen.
There will be a glorious vessel piloted skillfully.
The leader will always win.

In the beginning, middle and end of the show
there will be a commercial
telling you what to buy
in order to take this world home.

Joker: Year One

-October 30th-

It's been months of days at the library.
Learning all there is to know about
how to make napalm from Nerf foam
mixed with lighter fluid,
the Zimbadro Prison Experiment,
and the Gotham City PD's standard procedures
in case of natural disaster or terrorist attack.
Soaks it up like fresh gauze.

Years of weeks in the city dump.
Shooting strays with assault rifles
so his arms grow accustomed to recoil.
Sparring with winos until he can drive
a hood ornament through an eye socket
in one smooth action.

In his room, explosions in bloom
are tacked on all the walls. In the center
he sits cross legged. Holds his hand
a few inches above a portable blowtorch.
Learns to keep it there just a little longer each
time.

-January 13th-

After the third liquor store, realizes
he might as well just walk in with the gun out.
It's the way he moves through the room.
Dogs shudder, children cry, plants wince.
Even without the make-up, even before they see
the scars, the victim knows something sharp
and wet is about to happen.

After the fourth stash house,
decides regular crews are for regular crooks.
When they leave him in the Narrows,
icy boots ringing his ears, snow sticking
to his bloody lips, he vows to not work
with anyone he doesn't plan on shooting.
Smirks at how quick
a broken face teaches a lesson.

-April 1st-

He's been up for days. Eyes sunk
back like eight balls, teeth rotting yellow
with plaque, hands rattling in happy jitters.
It was supposed to be a quick penthouse invasion
over Easter weekend
but things got complicated.

You would be surprised how many
so-called "bad men" get skittish
when Grandma starts to gargle
from a box cutter slice cross the wind pipe.
How a hardened criminal just melts
at the first application of a hot stovetop.

Guys like that never understand.
It's not about the money,
it's about the half-second
when the prey's eyes
turn from terror wide
to numb thin.

It will be Tuesday morning soon.
There is a hundred dollar
meat cleaver in the kitchen
that has yet to be used to split a bone.

He knows he's on to something,
but hasn't found a face
for it yet. Can't decide
on what shape the ghost
of this story should take.

A little girl's muffled scream
shakes through duct tape. Blood
back splatters an arching smile
on her cheek. He thinks yes, yes,
this is the look we are going for.

-July 3rd-

Birth certificate, social security card
and every picture ever taken of him are ash
in the bottom of a bath tub.
Remembers last summer, before all this all started
when he first heard the rumor about the demon
that haunts the wicked. Still has the newspaper
clipping. Mob boss splayed on a searchlight
like a split chicken. Keeps it folded in
his breast pocket. A love letter.
Wanted poster. Report card
to aspire to.

Hones the edge of his knives and bullets
for tonight's double homicide robbery.
Plays solitaire with his calling cards.
The ones people weed out of the deck
when they want to keep the game predictable.

-September 27th-

Standing on the corner of Fifth and Main waiting
for disposable accomplices the mask dangles
from his fingers like a severed head.

Truck screeches to a halt, he gets in,
barely able to contain the laughter.

This is the end of the beginning.

Song for Trent Lott, Part 3

When Strom Thurmond ran for president,
we voted for him. We're proud of it.
And if the rest of the country
had followed our lead, we wouldn't have had
all these problems over the years.

                    -Trent Lott

What part of Segregation do you not understand?

Do you think they just hang themselves?
Were politely asked
to piss in a different bathroom
and that was all it took?

How do you think destiny manifests?

There is no difference
between a wall and a fist.
If you draw a line in red dirt,
there must be someone who is always ready
to cut off whatever crosses it.

On every protest march and project house.
Every reservation and border town.
Who do you think drains
all these swamps for you?

Do you know part of ourselves we sold
at the auction block
to stay on the loose side of the rope?

While you dream the impossible dream
of whiteness, we are the ones
who change your sheets

and they will never find a sleep
as sound as yours.

The Klansman who burns the cross
will forever see soot under his nails.
The skinhead's scalp will always rattle
even after the hair grows back.

The mill's stone knows its weight,
even if the one who turns the wheel doesn't.

To train a bloodhound to kill, you must beat it
every day with the buckle end of your belt.

What hot coal we hold under our tongues
ready for any uppity moment?
What heart's music is a chain gang clink?
What bullet we keep in what chamber?

Do you know what we do in the dark?
Understand when the loop of rope
is around a man's neck,
the mule kick can shatter a jaw.

How the foot begins to bend
into the Calvary boot
after the heel has been driven
into the head of a Lakota infant?

What Columbine carbine
do you think you can wield
like a bouquet
in your peach skin hand?

What Abu Ghraib
pyramid of flesh
has been erected

in your honor?

What son of McVeigh
is in the basement
of your federal building
with a bomb and a flag?

The monsters you made
to fight the race war you lost
are beginning to eat your children.

Can you imagine
the problems
if you won?

Dear Matt

Somewhere inside me
it is still that day in August.
Three Crips leave six different gray footprints
on my white Dead Kennedys tee shirt.
I'm sitting shotgun in your Taurus, purple ink
spreading under my left eye, the right side
of my jaw swelling like a balloon filled with spit.
I have never written a poem. You have not
collected a skyscraper of stolen stereos
on your bedroom floor. I haven't stopped
returning your pages. You haven't been pulled
over and covered the hoods of two police cursers
with your collection of weapons. I haven't been
on television for the poem I wrote about the fight.
You haven't enlisted. I haven't gone
back to school. You haven't reenlisted.
I haven't moved to a home so safe the only shots
in the air are sent from fingertips and are intended
as congratulations. I haven't received
an email that you have been killed in combat
from my ex girlfriend whose house
you helped me move out of. Matt,
somewhere inside myself all my clothes
still have spikes on every available surface.
What I have to say got me kicked
in the mouth. What I have to say
will get me flown across the world.
The bullet that kills you hasn't been
manufactured yet. My face is becoming
unrecognizable in your rearview mirror.
You tell me about the nickel-plated .44
you have under your mattress.
I tell you it's cool, but thanks.
Matt, I tell you thanks.

The show must go on

I once co-starred in a low-budget heist movie
about three slackers who rob a cannabis club,
shot without permits in the cuts of West Oakland.
Our prop bag included 3 Airsoft pistols, a leaky
gas mask and a bullet proof vest with a hole in it.
The day's agenda began with a 8 am call to set
to watch the cameraman for 3 hours.
Then director required us to walk
up and down an abandoned side street
like the automated targets in a shooting gallery.
The kids camped in front of the lone liquor store
looked at us like we were the craziest
white people they had ever seen. Around noon,
a gaggle of cops swooped down on a nearby
parking lot with news vans in their wake.
As an officer strung the yellow tape
we hid our equipment and asked what happened.
He said a toddler was found in the dumpster.
Eventually they left and we kept filming,
but our shadows kept getting longer and longer
as the sun set. This ruined what's called
the continuity. None of the footage could be used.
It was easy to tell the scenes didn't happen
in the order they appear.

Conversation with student regarding the nature of violence

When he said *Damn,* he dragged the flat *a* sound
out for ten solid seconds. The Sidekick
in his hand flicked open like a royal flush.
In it's grainy frame a girl no older than 14
jagged capital V cut into the whole length
of her chestnut face. My questions rush him
like children to a summer time playground.
I feel the cue to say something deep,
but I get off on being the bearer of bad news too.
Collector of murderabelia
and serial killer bedtime stories.
Why do I love sting of what shouldn't be seen?
The stare at the sun for a second too long.
The shock wears off like sugar. Flat metal bite
of chain link fence.   *For real though,*
he says, *that's fucked up.*
She's gonna wear shit that for life.

and I think of myself as a good person.

The box said "Snap Dragons" and only cost
a dollar. Sperm-shaped tissue paper pouches
that bit the air with cap-gun crack when thrown.
Only slightly louder than squeezing bubble wrap,
but still endlessly fascinating to our wet ears.
That summer, San Jose installed a light rail
system and it was free weekends.
There was a county fair in a mall parking lot.
We were big enough to go on our own,
but too small to be out after dark.
All the way there, we hopped off at every stop
to practice our ninja throws at the newspaper
boxes and the feet of old people. We laughed
so hard our cheeks ached. Down to our last few
rounds when we reached the fair, so naturally
we needed to drop them from some great height.
At the top of the Ferris wheel, we ignored
the orange wash around us. We couldn't even
hear the sound from that high up. Excited by even
the possibility of making a noise somewhere.
As the ride slowly jerked us down, I watched
a mother petting the back of a little girl.
A green tear streaked dinosaur speared down
her cheek. Small hand cupped over the eye.
Mouth arched in horror, as if the sky
had actually fallen on her.
What about that sound was so intoxicating?
How could no one tell we were the guilty?
Does it matter if we were back before nightfall?

My Nemesis

My Nemesis
just closed a deal
with Mountain Dew
to produce a new
malt liquor energy drink
that 50 Cent
will promote
on his world tour.

My Nemesis drives
a very expensive car
he could tell you a lot about.
His clothes are tailored,
but he buys whatever
the mannequins are wearing.

Sitting next to him
is a woman who thinks
that the best way
to fame and fortune
is through his cock.

There are very few pictures
of my Nemesis growing up.
He found himself to be
a very ugly child. However,

he still wears his high school
class ring. Birthstone- Sapphire.
Claims it *keeps his head
in the youth market.*

My Nemesis' business cards
say only his name and number.
If you ask, he will tell you

titles are for land,
not gentlemen.

At the stop light
he will ask her
to open her blouse
and remove her left breast.

He will take a make up case
from his pocket and scoop
a small serving of cocaine
on her nipple.

My Nemesis does not know
that this woman's cousin
did this exact same thing
on her 13th birthday,

nor would it
give him pause
if he did.

My Nemesis grew up
five blocks from me
in a slightly nicer house.
Whenever he waited for the bus,
it arrived.

93

The Notebook

is standard issue school marble. On the inside
cover she has listed the names of all her friends
killed this year, so far. A dozen deep,
each with a date of birth and death
not more than twenty years apart.

My first thought is an odd jealousy.
White people don't make memorial tee-shirts
for their young dead. When I was her age
I made sure no adult in my blast radius
noticed when someone I loved dissolved
in my hands. There are few things I believe in
that I cannot hold. One is the promise
of the written word. That which rattles in us
like a bullet in a glass jar will be silenced
if we fill it with our own sound. There is magic
in what locks trauma to page. It is the pull
of a splinter from under a nail.
A show to the small and immediate world
the similarities between all palms.

I'm staring at the book. She has decided
to never throw herself another birthday
party because someone was shot at the last one.
My feelings on this are irrelevant.
She wants to know what I think of the poem.
I tell her *it's good, but this line, where you say*
the funeral felt like a quiet nightmare,
you could get more specific.
It should be clear to someone
who has never been there
exactly what this feels like.

Appendix

Author's Note: *This absurdly long appendix was inspired by Nick Flynn's "Ticking is the Bomb." I loved the idea of a book having hyperlinks to more information about the work. I also know that most people who buy poetry books either facilitate or participate in writing workshops, so I thought it would be interesting to include some ideas about how to build prompts and discussion topics with the work. Please feel free to use them and be in touch if anything interesting comes out.*

-GKT

Murder Stay Murder is a line of dialogue taken from the television series "The Wire." A homicide detective (Bunk Moreland) is interviewing a thief (Omar Little) who robs drug dealers. The Omar has agreed to testify against an enforcer of a local cartel as revenge for killing Omar's boyfriend. While Bunk and Omar are talking, they realize they attended the same high school. Bunk asks Omar if he has any leads on any other murders, Omar asks, "going back how far." Bunk replies "going back as far as you need, murder stay murder."

Mad in the blood is a taken from a lyric in the Amanda Palmer song, "Runs in the Family"

Another Matter Entirely

Consider a social situation where you are forced to adhere to rules that you do not agree with.

What are the ways to enable or facilitate these cultural norms? What are the ways to violate this norm? What are the consequences of that violation?

This poem first appeared in the print journal *12th Street*.

It was inspired by the video blogs of Jay Smooth. www.illdoctrine.com

My first time all the way with a girl

Think of a rite of passage you underwent that gave you a new social status. List three objects that defined you at that time. Describe one scene from a movie or TV show you saw at the time. Who did you want to tell about this newfound status? What are three things you can't remember?

The Hottest Places

Describe the most "hellish" place you can imagine. How does it smell? What are the walls made of? Think of a time when you betrayed someone. What punishment do you deserve for your crime?

This poem first appeared in the print journal *Breadcrumb Scabs*.

Chuck

Who is the smallest person you know? Were they always that size? How did they get that way? Make a place for them to be big. Populate that

place with at least three treasures.
This poem first appeared in the print journal
Uphook.

My high school graduation

Consider a rite of passage where you were
present in flesh, but not in spirit. It could be your
rite, or one you are witnessing. Describe three
props or items used in that rite. Describe a flaw in
each prop.

This poem first appeared in the online journal
The Legendary.

Almaden and Foxworthy

Think of the last time you felt trapped.
Think of a house or neighborhood that personifies
this feeling. Describe one room in this place.
One person. One light source. What did you learn
from this place? What did it cost you?

This poem first appeared in the print journal
Uphook.
It is also part of the multi-voice poem with
Jamie DeWolf.

Of Copper and Chipped Teeth

Think of an act of violence you have witnessed.
This act can be accidental or intentional, but it
should be witnessed first hand. A dog that
snapped at you in real life is better than a terrorist
act you watched on Television. Name three
metals you associate with this act. Imagine
yourself at the perpetrator. What do you want a

witness to understand? Imagine yourself as the victim. What would you curse on the perpetrator?

This poem first appeared in the print journal
The Worcester Review.
It also appeared on HBO's Def Poetry Jam in Season 3.

27th and San Pablo

Think of an altercation between two people in a relationship. Compare one to a machine, one to an animal. Remember or invent a quote from each. In the place where the altercation occurred, what else happened?

This poem first appeared in a print edition of *Underground Voices.*

The Ghost of Tony Montana Haunts Martin Luther King Boulevard

Choose a fictitious hero or villain. Place them in the real world. Describe the place they loved most as a child. Describe a building or street they would fear most in the real world. What would be a fate worse then death?

This poem first appeared in the online journal
The Nervous Breakdown.

First day on the ward

Remember or construct a person who is your opposite in some way. If you are young, they are old, etc. Remember or create a conversation with them where you are speaking in stylistic opposites. If they are long winded, you are curt, etc. Before the end of the poem, admit to a lie you represent.

This poem first appeared in the online journal *Borderlands*.

Where did I get my sense of humor?

Think of the most offensive joke you know. Talk about the first time you heard it. Explain why it's funny.

War all the time is the name of Bukowski's collected poems from 1981-1984.

Man's Ruin

Choose a part of your body involved in your sex life. What would it be if it were a weather pattern? What would you sacrifice to it? How would it try to kill you?

This poem first appeared in the print journal *Breadcrumb Scabs*.

Thursday September 13, 2001

Remember where you were during a national tragedy. Remember a personal crisis that was happening at the same time. Choose a color that represents both. Describe as many shades of that color in as many places as you can.

The line "year of the orphan" is from the Aesop Rock song "9-5ers Anthem".

This poem first appeared in the print anthology *Don't Blame the Ugly Mug.*

Gomer Pyle's rifle writes a love letter

Choose an object from a work of fiction. This object should be crucial to the story, but not a focus. Not the ring to rule them all, but Frodo's sword. How does this object see the narrative unfold? How does it feel about its owner?

This poem first appeared in the online journal *Borderlands.*
It was inspired by Rob Ager's essay "The Hidden Hand."

Back to the front

Consider someone you love to hate, or hate to love. What have they taught you? What is the most vulnerable you have seen them? How have you failed them?

The title is taken from the Metallica song by the same name.

This poem first appeared in the online journal *The Legendary.*

Atticus Finch cuts a switch for Alberto Gonzales

Choose a hero from any work of fiction. List five things they would not consider heroic. Choose a person from the real world that is the opposite of this hero. What is the cruelest thing the hero could say?

Atticus Finch is the protagonist of the book and film "To Kill a Mocking Bird" by Harper Lee. Alberto Gonzales was the Attorney General during the George W Bush's administration and is often regarded as partially responsible for the use of torture by the United States.

Authorized Interrogation Techniques

The form of this poems is taken from Falu's "Say."

Consider the most brutal act one human can do to another. Elaborate on the most banal details of each action. What could or has been said to justify the act?

The actions described in this poem are taken directly from the Central Intelligence Agency's list of acceptable interrogation techniques.

South of Heaven

Consider a practitioner of a brutal act. It can be the one you wrote about in "Authorized", but it doesn't have to be. What were they like in High school? What was their favorite song? Now imagine them five years after the brutal act. How do they get through their day?

This poem first appeared in the online journal *The Legendary*.

You can find more information on music as torture at http://www.zerodb.org/

50 seconds in the life of a killer

When you think of the word "thug", who is the first person that comes to your mind? Name three things they have loved, three things they have destroyed, and three activities they enjoy. Set a timer to go off every thirty seconds. Begin writing as many specific details about this person or their life as you can, enumerating each. When the timer goes off, begin another number, even if it's mid sentence or word.

This poem is after *50 Years in the Career of an Aspiring Thug* by Susanne Wise.

The italicized portions are from *Hypnotize* by Christopher Wallace.

This poem first appeared in the online journal *Borderlands*.

An ongoing list of things I have learned from murderers.

Make a list of 5 people you know that have something in common. You should not have this thing in common with them. Write a secret you know about each. What object would represent that secret? Tell me something I wouldn't know about the object just by looking at it.

This poem first appeared in the online journal *SOFTBLOW*.

Drug Czar

Think of an authority figure you have no respect

for. Name three objects that are important to them and three things they will never know about you. What is the most disappointing sound you can imagine?

This poem first appeared in the online journal *Muzzle*.

How do you plead is intended as both a question of "guilty" or "not guilty" and as well as how the act of pleading is done.

In the Cannabis Club

Describe a place where an action is allowed that is normally not. What is on the walls? What does the furniture look like? Name one privilege you have that makes your life easier every day. Bring a person into this place, in spirit or flesh, that does not have this privilege.

No Homo Ghazal

A ghazal is a form of poem where there is a repeating phrase or word at the end of each line. Half of the fun in writing them is discovering new ways to use the repeating word.
Some fun ways to get at a good word are to think about –
-the word that goes on your headstone.
-the word that is your reality show middle name (aka "the situation").
- your favorite profanity.
- your favorite verb.
- the most dangerous object you can think of.
- the title of your favorite relative (mother, brother).

- your favorite season.
- a word you say more then 5 times a day.
- a part of your body you hate.
- a word that confuses you.
- a word you wish someone would call you.
- the word you hope no one ever calls you.

This poem first appeared in the print journal *Birdsong*.

Powder Burn

Consider a crime you have committed or contemplated committing. Who could or does commit this crime with the opposite effect you could or do experience. If this crime were a light source, what would it be?

This poem first appeared in the online journal *The November 3rd Club*.

Hymen Roth's Advice for Bernie Madoff On The Day of His Sentencing

Choose a villain from fiction and a villain from the real world who are guilty of essentially the same crime. Have one give the other three pieces of advice. The giver of advice should tell a story that he is ashamed of.

Hymen Roth is a character in "The Godfather, Part 2". He is modeled after one of the founding figures in organized crime, Myer Lansky.

This poem first appeared in the online journal *Underground Voices*.

Lesson Plan

A pantoum is a poetic form where the 2nd and 4th line of one stanza become the 1st and 3rd of the next. For this pantoum, think of a situation where a commonly held belief is proved false. What force of nature does this belief remind you of? Incorporate two direct quotes from people in this situation.

This poem first appeared in the online journal *Word Riot.*

The wax bullet tweets.

Choose an object that is used in the death of a person. The death can be intentional or accidental. The object can be directly involved or tangential. How does the object see the death? What does it know that the human actors don't? For an extra challenge, try to fit each of the objects statements into a communication medium that has a specific cadence. What would the atomic bomb say over telegraph? What does a Blackhawk helicopter gchat about?

How the guidance counselor used his words today

Think of a time when you betrayed someone. Tell the story using only 24 words. Now cut it down to 12. Now cut it down to 6. Now retell the story using as many words as you like, but make the 6 words said or thought by someone in the story.

This poem first appeared in the online journal *Pemmican.*

The rules of on screen engagement

Start with one of the basic archetypes for any plot (hero, villain, sidekick). List five of the rules for that archetype. Describe how these rules change when the race or gender of the archetype changes.

This poem first appeared in the online journal *Pemmican.*

The Making of a Socially Acceptable Sociopath

The film "Natural Born Killers" inspired this poem. The main antagonist, Jack Scagnetti, mentions in passing that he became interested in perusing serial killers after Charles Whitman murdered his mother.

Choose a character from fiction whose origin is alluded to, but not explicitly illustrated. Describe one toy from their childhood and one thing they felt guilty about. Describe an important day in this characters life, but list 5 things they don't remember.

This poem first appeared in the online journal *The Legendary.*

The man he intended to shoot.

Consider a crime were someone was unintentionally killed. It can be a real or fictitious. List 3 things that the killer wants to accomplish in his life. List 3 things the victim came in to physical contact with in his life. Tell the story of the victim the day before the killing and the killer, the day after.

This poem first appeared in the online journal *Union Station Magazine*.

Dirty Harry speaks to a 6th grade classroom at Througood Marshal Elementary

Choose an action hero you watched in your youth. Now age them to just before they could retire. Now place them in a world where all their former strength and bravery is meaningless.

This poem first appeared in the online journal *The Legendary*.

When I posted the poem about the locker room fistfight on Facebook

Take a subject from another poem you have written. Imagine this subject sitting next to you right now. What did you leave out of the other poem that they need to understand?
What do you regret about you real life relationship with them? What can you offer to make a mends?

Tooth for a tooth is a reference to Leviticus 24:20, "Fracture for fracture, eye for eye, tooth for tooth. As he has injured the other, so he is to be injured."

Ars Poetica

An ars poetica is poet's statement on the nature of poetry.

If all your poems were used as the basis for a

movie script, describe 3 scenes in that movie. They can be images and themes that regularly make appearances in your work, but should be different takes on them. Also, answer these questions-What are poems capable of affecting in the world? When are they not capable of doing this?

What I learned while teaching workshops in Rikers Island

Think of a place you hate. What gods watch over it? What would the furniture say if it could speak? What things are of value in this place? What advice would you give to someone going there for the first time?

Untitled.

This poem was based on a prompt from Rachel Mckibbens' blog at RachelMckibbens.com.

The masturbation session that stands out most to me

What is the most embarrassing situation that you have ever been caught in? Describe 3 tactile sensations you associate with it. What was the soundtrack? What changed after you were caught?

My first time all the way with a guy

Describe a rite of passage you have participated in where the participation of another person was essential. Describe the room where it took place. What was the furniture like? What did this other person not know about you? What would have been different if they had found out?

They are action figures, not dolls.

Choose on of your favorite toys from childhood. Explain them as if you were talking to someone who grew up in a culture where this toy didn't exist. List 5 lessons you learned from it. They can be positive or negative, intentionally or accentual. What do you wish you could unlearn?

Joker: Year One

Think of an iconic fictitious villain whose creation story you know very well. Invent five moments in this characters life. These moments can be larger or small, but each must contain one fluid, one sound and have taught this character something important.

This poem was heavily influenced by Heath Legder's portrayal of the Joker in the film "The Dark Knight". The title is a reference to "Batman- Year One" by Frank Miller.

This poem first appeared in the print journal *12ᵗʰ Street*.

Song for Trent Lott, Part 3

This poem is after *Song for Trent Lott* and *Song for Trent Lott, Part 2* by Roger Boniar-Agard.

Choose a poem written by someone else and write a sequel that speaks from a perspective alluded to in the poem but not explicitly addressed. Choose 5 images form the original poem and repurpose them for yours. The images should be altered, but still have the same basic tone.

This poem first appeared in the online journal *Underground Voices.*

Dear Matt

Similar to the "When I posted the poem on Facebook..." prompt, choose a person you have know who has been a subject of your poems. If you could only tell someone one moment of your relationship to explain it, what would that moment be? Describe what you were wearing. What else was happening in your life? What are you grateful for from the relationship?

This poem first appeared in the online journal *Muzzle.*

The show must go on.

Choose two different violent crimes, one fictitious, one real. Tell the story of each, with opposite aesthetics. If one is public, the other should be private. If one is loud, the other should be silent. End with your response to each, no more then one sentence.

This poem first appeared in the online journal *SOFTBLOW* and is alluding to the film "Smoked".

Conversation with student regarding
the nature of violence

Describe something you are fascinated by, but
feel guilty about the fascination. Compare it's
shape to a number or letter. Compare it to a food.
Compare it to a type of building material. Used a
quote from someone who has a similar
fascination.

This poem first appeared in the print journal
Birdsong.

and I think of myself as a good person

Think of a transgression you committed as a child
and still feel guilty about. What was it louder
than? What would it be if it were a type of
transportation? If you had to ask your child self 3
questions about the incident, what would they be?

This poem first appeared in the online journal
SOFTBLOW.

My Nemesis

This poem was written off a prompt form Marty
McConnell. www.martymcconnell.com

This poem first appeared in the online journal
SOFTBLOW.

The Notebook

If you could only be one object, what would it
be? Place this object in a real situation you have
experienced. If this object had a voice, what

would it sound like? What part of the body does this object act like? If you could use this object to teach someone a lesson, what would that lesson be?

This poem first appeared in the online journal *Pemmican.*

So many thanks to...

all the editors of the journals where these poems
first appeared. Mahogany Browne. Rico Frederick.
Omar Holman. Patrick Rosal. Sage Francis. Bamuthi.
Daphne Gottlieb. Emily Kagan Trenchard. Maureen
Benson. Marty McConnell. Rachel McKibbins.
Corrina Bain. Jamie DeWolf. Rupert Estanislao.
Jeffrey McDaniel. Roger Bonair Agard. Rebecca Hart.
Cate Marvin. Sigrid Nunez. Madge McKeithen.
Elizabeth Gaffney. Paul Violi. Charles Ellik. Sarton
Wienraub. Tongo Eisen-Martin. The louderARTS
project. The Bowery Poetry Club. The Riggio Writing
and Democracy Program. Urban Word NYC. Youth
Speaks. The Oakland Poetry Slam. The Positive
Health Project. Dance Theater Workshop. The Hip
Hop Theater Festival. Tourettes Without Regrets.

Geoff Kagan Trenchard's poems have been published in numerous journals including Word Riot, The Nervous Breakdown, The Worcester Review, SOFTBLOW and Pemmican. He has received endowments from the National Performance Network, Dance Theater Workshop, The Zellerbach Family Foundation and the City of Oakland to produce original theatrical work. As a mentor for Urban Word NYC, he taught weekly poetry workshops in the foster care center at Bellevue as well as in Rikers Island with Columbia University's "Youth Voices on Lockdown" program. He is a recipient of a fellowship from the Riggio Writing and Democracy program at the New School and the first ever louderARTS Writing Fellowship. He has performed poetry on HBO's Def Poetry Jam, at universities throughout the United States, and in theaters internationally as a member of the performance poetry troupe The Suicide Kings. He is currently a Juris Doctor Candidate for the class of 2014 at the Hofstra University School of Law.
He lives in Brooklyn and can be found at kagantrenchard.com.

Penmanship Poets

Joshua Bennett	*Jesus Riding Shotgun*
Mahogany L. Browne	*#Dear Twitter: Swag*
Michael Cirelli	*Everyone Loves The Situation*
Sean Patrick Conlon	*The Pornography Diaries*
Eboni Hogan	*Grits*
Zora Howard	*Clutch*
William Evans	*In the Event You are Caught Behind Enemy Lines*
Adam Falkner	*Ten for Faheem*
Barbara Fant	*Paint, Inside Out*
Falu	*10 Things I Want To Say To a Black Man*
Dasha Kelly	*Hershey Eats Peanuts*
Carvens Lissaint	*The Inspiration From: Heart To: Page*
Justin Long-Moton	*Manual*
Jaha Zainabu	*The Corners of My Shaping*
Lauren Zuniga	*The Nickel Tour*

www.PenmanshipBooks.com